Active Comprehension

4

Charlie Walker

Oxford University Press

Contents

Note to Teachers

Active Comprehension is a series of four reading comprehension and composition books for primary English classes. *Active Comprehension* takes an active approach to reading comprehension. In each book the pupils are exposed to a variety of types of reading passages and activities, comprehension exercises and composition exercises. The books have been designed to turn reading and writing into interesting, enjoyable and skill building activities for the pupils.

1 Pre-reading

Before reading a text, it is a good idea to get pupils thinking about the topic, to arouse their interest and curiosity, or to prepare them for new vocabulary. In most units, some sort of pre-reading activity or task is provided. These can be supplemented with general discussion or more direct work on vocabulary if the teacher thinks it would be helpful.

2 Reading texts

Pupils are exposed to a variety of different types of texts in *Active Comprehension*. As the pupil moves up in the series, he or she will be required to identify more explicitly the type of text it is and even produce writing in this style. However at the lower levels, the most important thing is to build the pupils' skills and confidence in deciphering any type of text they come across.

The texts have been written to give pupils exposure to different types of writing and also to appeal to the interests and tastes of different pupils. It is very important when teaching reading comprehension to encourage a positive attitude towards reading. Reading should be presented as a lively and exciting activity which opens up the world to the pupil. The pupils' **curiosity** should be aroused and used to create as much enthusiasm for reading as possible. Pupils should be encouraged to read outside the classroom and **supplementary materials** should be available for pupils to use independently.

Some teachers will want to use the text to ask pupils to **read aloud**. This is a useful thing to do from time to time as long as the rest of the class remains interested and attention is not diverted away from understanding the text to pronunciation practice. It is also useful to allow the pupils to read silently on their own and then read the text aloud to go over any difficulties with it. It is also good to encourage pupils to discuss the text in their own words.

Sometimes the texts will contain **vocabulary** which will be new to the pupils. This is because learning to understand new words through **context** is an important part of learning to read. 'Context' can mean from the words around it, from the general logic of the story or from the illustrations that go with it. Sometimes this involves a certain amount of guessing and this is an important part of learning. Pupils can also be encouraged to learn to use dictionaries, to start their own dictionaries/word lists and also to enlist the teacher's help when they do not know a word.

3 Comprehension and composition exercises

A wide variety of comprehension exercises is provided. These exercises are designed to exploit the pupils' basic understanding of the text, to train them to infer information from the text, to encourage them to bring their own knowledge and experience to their perception of the text, and to widen the range of language and style which they can understand and use.

For levels 1 and 2 the exercises focus more on comprehension with limited composition exercises. At levels 3 and 4, increased emphasis is placed on the pupils' ability to recognise and produce different types of writing and the amount of composition work is increased.

The exercises are designed so that they can be used individually, in pairs or as a class. It is often useful to encourage focused classroom discussion and activity on the exercises and texts. It is also helpful to encourage pupils to bring their own experiences to the comprehension and composition work when it is appropriate.

First aid

1 Match the pictures to the words in the box.

plaster   bandage   eye patch   sling   crutches
plaster cast   sting   antiseptic cream

_____   _____   _____   _____

_____   _____   _____   _____

2 Look at the picture below. Can you match the sentences to the pictures? The first one is done for you.

a   He's **twisted** his **ankle**.
b   She's **grazed** her knee.
c   He's broken his arm.
d   He's cut his eye.
e   She's broken her leg.
f   He's cut his finger.

3 Read the text and then answer the questions.

Charlotte was given a new bicycle for her birthday. But it turned out to be not such a happy birthday. A motorbike drove past so close to her that she cycled up on to the pavement and fell.

Poor Charlotte couldn't move her right leg. The bike had fallen on top of it. It was badly cut and broken. A man rushed to call an ambulance. She was taken to the hospital, where a doctor put her leg in a **plaster cast**. After this, Charlotte had to walk on **crutches** for four weeks until she had the plaster cast removed.

1 What was Charlotte doing when the accident happened?
2 How was she hurt?
3 Who called the ambulance?
4 What did the doctor do?
5 How long was it before she could walk normally?

4 Read what happened. Then use the words in the boxes to write what happened before.

on top of it   fall   bike   1 She hurt her leg.
The bike had fallen on top of it.

thief   steal   it   2 He lost his money.
_____

car   hit   it   3 The bike was broken.
_____

her   friends   go   4 She arrived too late.
_____

the boy   paint   it   5 The cat was blue.
_____

rain   the night before   6 Everything was wet.
it   _____

5 Look at the picture in exercise 2. Write about how each accident happened. Use your imagination to answer the following questions.

1 How did the accident happen?
2 Who was there to help?
3 How did the boy/girl feel?
4 Did he/she have to go to hospital?
5 How long was it before he/she felt better?

3

2 Bad habits

1 Which of these three things fit together? Can you say why?

a helping at home ☐
b always arriving late at school ☐
c not tidying up ☐
d eating too much ☐

2 Now read the text.

Bad habits

Almost everybody has some bad **habits**. A bad habit is something which is either not good for us, or not good for other people. One bad habit is making a **mess** and leaving it for someone else to **tidy up**. People may get angry if other people never wash up the dishes after they've used them, or if they always spend a lot of time in the bathroom while other people are waiting to use it. Can you think of habits that **annoy** you? For example, are you annoyed when people leave the lids off things? Does anyone in your house leave their shoes everywhere?

Some bad habits are not very **harmful**, but there are some that are bad for your health. Smoking is an example of a habit that is harmful both to the person who smokes and to the people who are sitting in the same room. It **damages** everybody's lungs. Can you think of any more habits like this?

Some people have bad habits outside the home. For example, they drop **litter** in the streets, which makes the place look untidy and unattractive for everybody. What other bad habits can you think of like this?

3 Find the questions in the text. Write the answers or tell them to your classmates.

1 Can you think of habits that annoy you?

2 _____

3 _____

4 _____

5 _____

4 Find these bad habits in the text and then write them below the

1 _____   2 _____

4

3 _____

4 _____

_____

6 Make a table with more examples of bad habits.

Bad habits at home	Other bad habits
Not tidying up your mess	

5 Do you think that the bad habits mentioned are serious, or not very important? Write them in the table below in the order of how bad they are. (7 = very very bad, 1 = not bad at all)

7	
6	
5	
4	
3	
2	
1	

Explain why you gave your scores.

For example: Not tidying up your mess I think this deserves 4 out of 7, because it s quite bad but not very very bad.

7 Questions which require a Yes/No answer are sometimes called closed questions. Look at the question below.

auxiliary   subject   infinitive

Do *you* *clean* *your teeth every night?*

1 The auxiliary is the helping verb. What auxiliary would we use in the simple past tense? What auxiliary would we use in the present perfect tense?

2 Using your examples from exercise 5, write a questionnaire about habits and interview someone else in the class.

For example:

Yes   No

1 Do you clean your teeth every night? ☐ ☐

2 Do you always replace the cap on the toothpaste? ☐ ☐

3 Jobs

1 Can you put these letters into order and find the jobs?

| rdotco | iptlo | iatx vidrer | eduig |

2 Read the descriptions of these four jobs to your partner. Read them one sentence at a time. How many sentences does your partner need before he can guess what each job is? Then write the job.

1 This person can be a woman or a man. She is somebody who listens carefully to people's problems. She **examines** our bodies to see if there is anything wrong. She works in a **surgery** or a hospital. She sometimes tells us to take medicines. She has to be patient and understanding. She works with sick people.

_____

2 This person can be a man or a woman. She is somebody who works with visitors to her country. She travels to famous places and **monuments**. She needs to know a lot of interesting facts about her country. She needs to be very patient and enjoy helping people. She speaks some foreign languages. She has to talk a lot.

_____

3 This person is usually a man, although it could be a woman. He is always moving on the roads. He usually works in a big city or town. He uses a **meter**. He may work at any time. He drives people to places.

_____

4 This job is usually done by a man. It's a very important job. He's **responsible** for everybody's safety. He leads a crew. He must have very good **eyesight**. He has to stay calm and think quickly in an emergency. He is often in the air. He wears a uniform.

_____

3 Complete these sentences.

1 A doctor is somebody who <u>helps us when we are sick.</u>

2 A pilot is somebody who <u>flies planes.</u>

3 A police officer is somebody who
_____

4 A vet is somebody who_____
_____

5 A dentist is somebody who _____
_____

6 A postman is somebody who_____
_____

7 A shopkeeper_____
_____

8 A teacher_____
_____

9 A waiter_____
_____

4 Read the texts in exercise 2 and answer these questions.

1 Who looks at you if you don't feel well? <u>the doctor</u>

2 Who must see well? _____

3 Who does not usually work in the countryside? _____

4 Who must keep people safe?
_____

5 Who has people working for him?
_____

6 Who must like talking to people in different languages? _____

7 Who knows about old buildings and statues? _____

5 Choose a job from exercise 3 (or another job) and write a description like the ones in exercise 2. Remember not to include the name of the job. You could write:

1 whether the job is done by a man or a woman
2 where the person works
3 what equipment the person uses
4 what sort of person the job needs

Let your partner guess the job.

A day in the life of Susan Collier

1 Look at the pictures in this story.
Then answer the questions.

1   Where do you think the woman lives?
2   What time of the year is it?
3   Is her dog just a pet? How does the dog help her?
4   Are other people helpful towards her?
5   What problems do you think she has in her daily life?

2　1　Now tell the story to your partner. Here are some words to help you. Ask your teacher if you don't know any of the words.

guide dog	patient	lead	careful
traffic	busy	blind	cross
guide	faithful	rely	wait

3　Complete this table with words from the box above.

Noun	Adjective	Verb
guide dog	busy	rely

Now see if you can match the words to any of the pictures in exercise 1.

4　Can you write the story of the blind woman's shopping trip? The first two sentences are done for you.

Susan Collier lives with her faithful dog, Bess. But Bess is not an ordinary dog.

5　Complete this conversation between Susan and the man at the bus stop. Use the words in the box.

patient	faithful	bus	rely
	name	guide	

Man:　Which 1_____ are you waiting for?

Susan:　The No.10 to Grove Road.

Man:　Your dog is very 2_____. What's her 3_____?

Susan:　She's called Bess. She's a good 4_____ dog. I 5_____ on her a lot.

Man:　She must be a 6_____ friend. Oh, here's our bus.

5 Sending a letter

1 Show how Jenny's letter gets to her cousin in Australia. Look at the pictures and then put the sentences in order.

a Jennifer's letter goes by **van** to the airport and is put on the plane. ☐

b Post-office workers put the mail into separate bags according to the country or area it is going to. ☐

c The postman or woman **delivers** the letter. ☐

d Jennifer puts her letter in the box. ☐

e When the plane arrives in Australia, the letters are **unloaded** into vans and taken to the local **sorting office**. ☐

f Small vans take the letters out to different delivery **areas**. ☐

g The postman empties the letter-box and takes the letters to the sorting office in his van. ☐

2 Can you match the words to their definitions? If you are not sure look at exercise 1 again.

sorting office	abroad
van	car used for transporting things
mail	a place where people put letters in categories
overseas	to take something to somebody
to deliver	letters or package

10

3

> The **passive form** is used when the person who is doing the action is not as important as the action itself. For example, in the sentence
>
> *The letters are **unloaded** into vans.*
>
> the important thing is the verb or action (***are unloaded***). It is not important **who** performs the action.
>
> The **passive** is formed by using the correct form of the verb '**to be**', followed by the past participle.

Put these sentences in the passive form.

1 The postman empties the letter-box.

   The letter-box _____

   _____

2 He takes the letters to the sorting office.

   The letters_____

   _____

3 Post-office workers sort the mail into different bags.

   The mail _____

   _____

4 Small vans take the letters out to different delivery areas.

   The letters _____

   _____ in small vans.

5 The local postman or woman delivers the letter.

   The letter _____

   by the local postman or woman.

4 When you write an address in English it is important to do it in the right order.

1	Name	Jennifer Robinson
2	Number and street	30 Mill Rd
3	Town	Dover
4	Area, county or state	Kent
5	Postal code	CT3 1GL
6	Country	GREAT BRITAIN

Can you write your own address according to the system above? Write your best friend's address too.

5 Write out this conversation putting in all the punctuation.

1 im writing a letter to my cousin said jennifer

   "I'm writing a letter to my cousin," said Jennifer.

2 where does your cousin live asked sarah

   _____

   _____

3 jennifer said she lives in australia her house is near the beach

   _____

   _____

4 how long will your letter take to get there asked sarah

   _____

   _____

5 about a week if it goes by plane said jennifer

   _____

   _____

6   A letter from Jamie

1   Read Jamie's letter.

Jamie Sugden
7 Kings Road
Edinburgh
Scotland
ED5 4FC

15 November 1995

Dear Ashraf

a   I am Jamie, from Scotland.

b   I'm 13 years old and I live in Edinburgh, the capital city of Scotland.

c   A lot of people think that Scotland is part of England, but it's not. It's a separate country, although both Scotland and England are part of the United Kingdom. Lots of things in Scotland are different, including our schools, some laws and even our **bank notes**. People visit Scotland to look at the beautiful scenery. We have mountains and **lakes**, which we call lochs. You may have heard about Loch Ness, where people say a **monster** lives.

d   I go to school five days a week, from Monday to Friday. We usually finish at about 4 o'clock, but I often stay behind to do **gym** or play football. My favourite subjects are English, History and Science.

e   On Saturday I play football for the school team, and on Sundays I usually go fishing with my dad. I love fishing, even though we don't often catch much.

f   Please write soon and tell me all about your life and your country.

Goodbye for now.

Jamie

12

2 Choose the best answer to these questions.

1 A **capital** city is
   a a small city ☐
   b an important city ☐
   c a city by a river ☐

2 Egypt, England and Turkey are
   a countries ☐
   b cities ☐
   c people ☐

3 A **law** is
   a a rule which must be obeyed ☐
   b a police officer ☐
   c a car ☐

3 True (T) or false (F)?

1 Scotland is part of the United Kingdom. ☐T

2 Some Scottish money is different from English money. ☐

3 There is definitely a monster in Loch Ness. ☐

4 Jamie likes History more than Science. ☐

5 Jamie and his dad catch a lot of fish. ☐

4 Can you match the following paragraph headings to the paragraphs in Jamie's letter?

Opening **greeting** ☐
My hobbies ☐
Ending ☐
About myself ☐
My country ☐
My school ☐

5 Put the words in these sentences in the right order.

1 part the England United Kingdom Scotland of are and

England and Scotland are part of
the United Kingdom.

2 lochs lakes called Scotland are in

_____

3 Jamie days school week goes five a to

_____

4 fishing football loves playing Jamie and

_____

6 Use the paragraph headings in exercise 4 to write a reply to Jamie's letter, or if you have a pen-friend of your own write a similar letter to him or her.

The rabbit's foot - part one

1 Some people think that some objects will bring them **luck**. Make a list of things that are supposed to bring luck. Compare your list with your partner's.

2 Now read the story.

Once upon a time there was an old woman who lived in a small house by a forest. She was very poor and spent her time **collecting** small **twigs** from trees in the forest to make into brooms. She sold the **brooms** for a living.

One day in winter, as night was falling, the old woman was still busy in the forest collecting twigs. She was very tired and cold.

"If I could make just one wish," she said, "I would wish for a nice new house and some bread and tea that would never **run out**. Then I wouldn't have to sell brooms any more."

She **sighed**, and carried on collecting twigs. Suddenly she saw a **hunter**, who held out a rabbit's foot to her.

"Here you are, old woman," he said. "Take this rabbit's foot, and when you are in your home, brush it across your table and make a wish. Your wish will **come true**. But don't forget that you can only have two wishes!" And then the hunter disappeared as quickly as he had arrived.

The old woman hurried home with her big bag of twigs on her **shoulder** and the rabbit's foot in her coat pocket. When she got inside her house she sat down at the table smiling. "This rabbit's foot is going to end all my problems," she said.

3 Don't look at the text. See how well you remember the story. Answer these questions.

1 What kind of a day was it?
_____

2 Did the woman have a happy life?
_____

Why/why not? _____
_____

3 How did the old woman make a living? _____
_____

4 How was she feeling when she met the hunter? _____
_____

5 How did she feel when she arrived home? _____
_____

4 Write questions for these answers.

1 <u>What did the old woman do to earn money?</u>
_____

She sold brooms.

2 _____
_____

A nice new house and some bread and tea that would never run out.

3 _____
_____

A rabbit's foot.

4 _____
_____

Two.

5 _____
_____

In her pocket.

5

In stories sometimes we need to know when people are speaking. We use these marks "..." before and after the speech.

1 Look at the text and <u>underline</u> the parts where people talk.

2 Look at the tenses. Which tense is the story in? Which tense is the speech in?

6 Before you read part two of the story, try to answer the following questions with your friends.

1 What do you think will happen?
_____
_____

2 What wishes will the woman make? _____
_____

3 Do you think the story will have a happy ending? _____
_____

Now write a paragraph to tell the end of the story. Use your own ideas. Remember to write in the past tense.

8 The rabbit's foot - part two

1 Match these words with their meanings.

make fun of	to turn on its head
upside down	silly
foolish	to laugh at someone

2 Read the text.

The old woman sat at the table with the rabbit's foot. She suddenly thought that the hunter had been **making fun of her**. Maybe he was just having a **joke** at a poor old woman's expense.

"It's probably good for nothing. A rabbit's foot indeed!" she thought to herself. She picked it up and brushed it across the table, saying with a smile, "I wish this house would turn itself **upside down**."

She **instantly** fell from her chair. The house was upside down! She looked up at the floor, which had become the ceiling, and down at the ceiling, which had become the floor.

"What a foolish old woman I am," she said. "Now I have only one wish, and what can I wish for? I'll just have to wish for my house to be the right way up again."

She **crawled** back to the table, which had fallen onto the ceiling, and brushing the rabbit's foot across it she said, "I wish this house would turn itself the right way up." And with that, the house immediately returned to the way it had been before.

So the old woman remained poor, and carried on going out into the forest to collect twigs for her brooms.

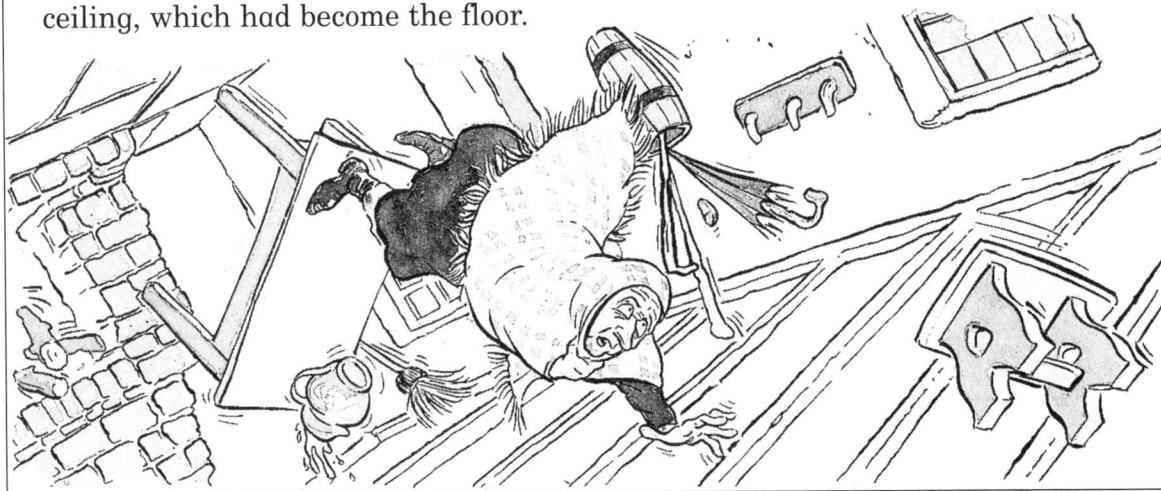

3 Here are the main events of the second part of the story. Can you put them in the correct order?

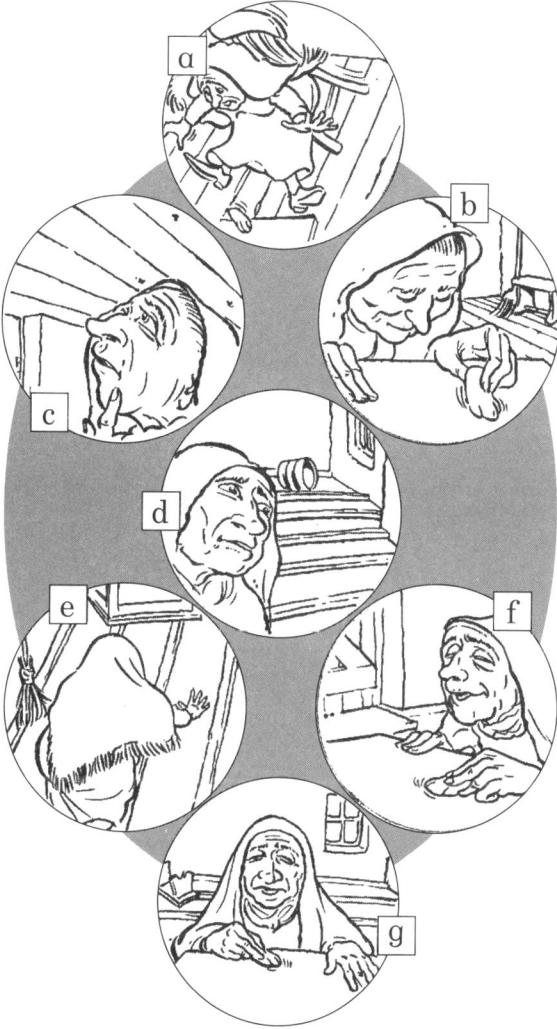

a She fell from her chair. ☐
b She brushed the rabbit's foot across the table. ☐
c She looked up at the floor. ☐
d She looked down at the ceiling. ☐
e She crawled to the table. ☐
f She made her first wish. ☐
g She made her second wish. ☐

4

When we make wishes, we use the verb '**to wish**'. If we wish for something to happen, we use '**would**' + the infinitive without '**to**'. For example, the old woman said '*I wish this house would turn itself upside down.*'

If we wish to have something, we can say, '*I wish I had a new house.*' Although we mean we wish to have it now, or in the future, we use the past tense.

What do you think of the woman's second wish? Think of three better wishes for the old woman.

"I wish _____

_____

I wish _____

_____

I wish _____

_____ "

5 This story is a **fairy tale**. A fairy tale is a special kind of traditional story. A fairy tale often starts with '*Once upon a time, there was ...*'.

1 Can you think of a fairy tale you know? Write a list of the main events and characters in the story.

Events	Characters

2 Now use your list to write a short fairy tale.

9 A dinosaur movie

1 Do you know all of the adjectives in this box? Check them with your partner, then put them into the correct gaps in exercise 2.

scientific happy amazing fantastic
successful frightening prehistoric

2 Read the text.

One of the most 1_____ film **directors** in Hollywood history is Steven Spielberg. His film *Jurassic Park* was a **box office** hit, filling cinemas all over the world. The film is about **dinosaurs**, not millions of years ago, but in the present day.

A **millionaire** finds a way to make dinosaurs using all the modern 2_____ knowledge and technology. He builds a big park in South America, where visitors will be able to come and see these 3_____ **creatures**.

A group of people, including the millionaire's two grandchildren, come to see round the 4_____ park. Things **go wrong**. The computers **controlling** the **gates** and **fences** break down, and the dinosaurs and other 5_____ animals escape and scare the visitors.

The film is both 6_____ and exciting, but like most Hollywood movies, there is a 7_____ ending.

3 Choose the best title for the text.

a The history of dinosaurs ☐
b An amazing movie ☐
c Steven Spielberg ☐

4

> We often use the expression *'One of the most...in the world/country/etc.'* when making superlative descriptions of things or people. Remember:
>
> **Most** + long adjective
> *Most successful*
>
> or
>
> short adjective + **est**
> *happiest*

Use 'One of the most...' to complete these descriptions. The words in the boxes will help you.

| big | expensive | famous | high | fast |

1 Mount Blanc is *one of the highest* mountains in the world.
2 Mexico City is _____ _____ cities in the world.
3 The diamond is _____ _____ stones in the world.
4 Omar Sharif is _____ _____ actors in the world.
5 The cheetah is _____ _____ animals in the world.

5 What do you think? Fill in the gaps.

1 _____ is one of the best pupils in the class.
2 _____ is one of the biggest shops in my neighbourhood.
3 _____ is one of the best football players in the school.
4 _____ is one of the funniest actors in the world.
5 _____ is one of the most famous places in my country.

6 Which tense is the description of the film written in?

> Often when we write about what happens in a book or film we write in the present tense.

Write a short description of a film you've seen. You'll need to include:
1 the name of the film
2 the names of the actors and director (if you know them)
3 a brief summary of the story

7 Now write the titles of four films you've seen or heard about, including the one you described in exercise 6. Ask your partner to read your description, and choose the correct title from your list.

A family holiday

1 Look at the pictures. Put a (circle) around the 15 words in the box that you think will be useful in telling the story of the Cook family's holiday.

countryside	dinosaur	**check in**	luggage
boat	badminton	guest house	put up
sea	**set off**	**roof rack**	tired
hotel	waiter	campsite	relax
perfect	storm	fall down	taxi

Answers

1 First aid

(1) plaster, bandage, antiseptic cream, sting, crutches, eye patch, plaster cast, sling

(3) 1 When the accident happened Charlotte was riding her new bicycle.
2 Charlotte hurt her right leg.
3 A man who saw the accident called the ambulance.
4 The doctor put her leg in a plaster cast.
5 It was four weeks before she could walk normally.

(4) 1 The bike had fallen on top of it.
2 A thief had stolen it.
3 A car had hit it.
4 Her friends had already gone.
5 The boy had painted it.
6 It had rained the night before.

2 Bad Habits

(1) b, c and d fit together because they are all bad things.

(3) 1 Can you think of habits that annoy you?
2 Are you annoyed when people leave the lids off things?
3 Does anyone in your house leave their shoes everywhere?
4 Can you think of any more habits like this?
5 What other bad habits can you think of like this?

(4) 1 not tidying up
2 spending a lot of time in the bathroom while other people are waiting to use it
3 smoking
4 dropping litter

(7) 1 Simple past tense auxiliary: did
Present perfect auxiliary: have

3 Jobs

(1) doctor, pilot, taxi driver, guide

(2) 1 doctor 2 guide
3 taxi driver 4 pilot

(3) 1 A doctor is somebody who helps us when we are sick.
2 A pilot is somebody who flies planes.
3 A police officer is somebody who makes sure people follow the law.
4 A vet is somebody who looks after the health of animals.
5 A dentist is somebody who looks after people's teeth.
6 A postman is somebody who delivers letters.
7 A shopkeeper is somebody who sells things in a shop.
8 A teacher is somebody who helps people learn.
9 A waiter is somebody who serves food in a restaurant.

(4) 1 The doctor 2 The pilot
3 The taxi driver 4 The pilot
5 The pilot 6 The guide
7 The guide

4 A day in the life of Susan Collier

(1) 1 The woman lives in a town.
2 It is winter.
3 The dog is a guide dog and helps the woman to 'see'.
4 Other people are usually helpful towards her.
5 Students' own answers.

(3) Nouns: guide dog, traffic, lead
Adjectives: patient, careful, busy, blind, faithful
Verbs: lead, cross, guide, rely, wait

(5) 1 bus 2 patient 3 name
4 guide 5 rely 6 faithful

5 Sending a letter

(1) a 4   b 3   c 7   d 1
    e 5   f 6   g 2

(2) sorting office: a place where people put
letters in categories
van: car used for transporting things
mail: letters or package
overseas: abroad
to deliver: to take something to somebody

(3) 1 The letter-box is emptied.
2 The letters are taken to the sorting
office.
3 The mail is sorted into different bags.
4 The letters are taken out to different
delivery areas in small vans.
5 The letter is delivered by the local
postman or woman.

(5) 1 "I'm writing a letter to my cousin,"
said Jennifer.
2 "Where does your cousin live?" asked
Sarah.
3 Jennifer said, "She lives in Australia.
Her house is near the beach."
4 "How long will your letter take to get
there?" asked Sarah.
5 "About a week if it goes by plane,"
said Jennifer.

6 A letter from Jamie

(2) 1 b   2 a   3 a

(3) 1 T 2 T 3 F 4 F 5 F

(4) a Opening greeting b About myself
c My country   d My school
e My hobbies   f Ending

(5) 1 England and Scotland are part of the
United Kingdom.
2 Lakes are called lochs in Scotland.
3 Jamie goes to school five days a week.
4 Jamie loves fishing and playing
football.

7 The rabbit's foot - part one

(3) 1 It was a cold day in winter.
2 The woman didn't have a happy life

because she was poor.
3 She made a living by making brooms
from twigs and selling them.
4 When she met the hunter she was
feeling very tired and cold.
5 She felt happy when she arrived home.

(4) 1 What did the old woman do to earn
money?
2 What did the old woman say she
would wish for if she had one wish?
3 What did the hunter give the woman?
4 How many wishes did the hunter
say the woman could have?
5 Where did the woman put the rabbit's
foot?

(5) 1 Pupils' own answers.
2 The story is in the past tense. The
speech is in the present tense.

8 The rabbit's foot - part two

(1) make fun of: to laugh at someone
upside down: to turn on its head
foolish: silly

(3) a 3   b 1   c 4   d 5
    e 6   f 2   g 7

9 A dinosaur movie

(1) 1 successful   2 scientific
3 amazing   4 fantastic
5 prehistoric   6 frightening
7 happy

(3) b

(4) 1 Mount Blanc is one of the highest
mountains in the world.
2 Mexico City is one of the biggest
cities in the world.
3 The diamond is one of the most
expensive stones in the world.
4 Omar Sharif is one of the most
famous actors in the world.
5 The cheetah is one of the fastest
animals in the world.

10 A family holiday

(2) After they had arrived at the campsite they all helped to put up the tent.

After dinner, Susan and David played badminton while their parents did the washing up.

The Cook family set off on their holiday with their tent and bags packed tightly on the roof rack.

In the evening they enjoyed a lovely meal which Susan and David had prepared earlier.

(3) 1 The Cook family set off on their holiday with their tent and bags packed tightly on the roof rack.
2 After they had arrived at the camp-site they all helped to put up the tent.
3 In the evening they enjoyed a lovely meal which Susan and David had prepared earlier.
4 After dinner, Susan and David played badminton while their parents did the washing up.

11 Food

(3) 1 f   2 b   3 a   4 g
5 d   6 c   7 e

(4) cavities: little holes in your teeth
additives: something added to food to give it more flavour or colour
raw: not cooked
frozen: as cold as ice
vitamins: something found naturally in food that is good for us

(5) a I like fast-food because I'm always in a hurry.
b If you eat too many sweets you will have to visit me often.
c Too much salt can cause troubles for your heart.
d If my children eat properly now they might not have problems later.

(6) 1 Too much salt is bad for us because it could damage our hearts.
2 Sugar is bad for our teeth because it can cause cavities.

3 Butter and oil are fats, and we should cut down on them.
4 Fresh salads are healthy and good for us.

12 Tony's day

(1) 1 present continuous
2 present simple
3 simple past

(3) 7.15 Tony's father wakes him up.
7.20 He eats breakfast.
7.30 He has a shower and gets dressed.
8.00 He leaves home.
8.10 The train comes in.
8.20 The train arrives at Faversham.
8.35 Tony arrives at school.
8.45 The school bell rings.
8.50 The school meeting begins.

(4) 1 c   2 a   3 b   4 b
5 b   6 b

13 Tony's school

(3) (top) register, tuck shop
(bottom) canteen/queue, assembly

(4) 1 a   2 c   3 a   4 b   5 a

14 The solar system

(1) There are nine planets in the solar system.

(3) Pluto – 5,900 (**247**)
Neptune – 4,497 (165)
Uranus – 2,870 (84)
Saturn – 1,427 (29)
Jupiter – 778 (11.9)
Mars – 228 (1.9)
Earth – 150 (1)
Venus – 108 (0.6)
Mercury – 58 (0.2)

(4) 1 further, larger   2 closer, longer
3 biggest

(5) 1 There are nine planets going around the sun.
2 Jupiter is the largest planet, while Pluto is the most distant from the sun.

3 The moon reflects the sun's light.

4 Two planets, Mercury and Venus, take less than a year to go round the sun.

15 Earthquakes - part one

(1) 1 Earthquakes happen when two plates in the earth's crust jerk against each other.

2 Earthquakes often cause damage to buildings.

3 Earthquakes occur in California because two plates meet at the San Andreas fault.

4 The size of an earthquake is measured on the Richter scale.

5 Not all earthquakes are felt by people.

6 Not many people died in the 1994 Los Angeles earthquake because it happened early in the morning.

(3) 1 F   2 T   3 F   4 T

16 Earthquakes - part two

(3) 1 a   2 a   3 c   4 c
5 b   6 b   7 a

17 Hobbies and spare time

(3) 1 I keep them in a stamp album.

2 My mother brings them home from work.

3 Coins are difficult to find because people hold on to their money.

4 Apart from collecting things I like playing volley ball and computer games.

5 One of my friends collects things like bottle tops and shoelaces.

(4) 1 How do you get the stamps off the envelopes?

2 Which are your favourite stamps?

3 Where do you get your coins from?

4 What does your friend do with her collection?

18 Kites

(3) Water activities: swimming, paddling, canoeing, rowing

Land activities: playing volleyball, sunbathing, flying a kite

(4) 1 1 wire   2 string   3 groove
4 joint   5 glue

19 Grammar

(3) Question: What is grammar?
Answer: Grammar is the way we put words together to say something that makes sense.

Question: The drive of the car fell asleep in his sitting. Two words are wrong here. What are they?
Answer: drive (driver) and sitting (seat)

Question: How should we say He the cake ate ?
Answer: He ate the cake.

Question: Can you think of some more nouns/verbs/adjectives?
Answer: Pupils' own answers.

(4) 1 Most kinds of fish lay huge numbers of eggs.

2 Finland has long cold winters and warm summers.

3 Many people work in the fishing industry on the coast of Ireland.

4 Giant pandas are some of the rarest animals in the world.

5 Louis Pasteur discovered that bacteria cause disease.

6 In the Middle East farmers grow cotton, tobacco and fruits such as dates, grapes, oranges and olives.

(5) Nouns: produce, word, earth, year, electricity, glass, attack, sand
Adjectives: good, slow, glass, rich, pure
Verbs: produce, build, attack, explode, move, put

(6) paragraph, noun, comma, verb, sentence, fullstop, capital letter, question mark, speech mark

20 _____

(2) 1 F   2 T   3 T   4 F
5 F   6 T   7 F

(3) 1 a   2 b   3 a   4 c

7

_____

_____

2 Match the first half of the sentences to their appropriate endings.

After they had arrived at the campsite

After dinner, Susan and David played badminton

The Cook family set off on their holiday

In the evening they enjoyed a lovely meal

while their parents did the washing up.

which Susan and David had prepared earlier.

they all helped to put up the tent.

with their tent and bags packed tightly on the roof rack.

3 Write each of the four sentences from exercise 2 beneath one of the pictures in exercise 1.

4 Complete the story by writing what happened in the other three pictures.

5 Write a short paragraph about a holiday you had or about a holiday you would like to have.

_____

_____

_____

_____

21

11 Food

1 Before you read the text, complete these food lists in the table.

3 types of fruit	banana, apple,
3 types of vegetable	
3 types of food with a lot of sugar	
3 types of food with a lot of salt	
3 types of food with a lot of butter or oil	

Now compare your lists with your partner or the class. Have you got any of the same things on your lists?

2 Read about food.

(a) These days many people eat **convenience food**. This means food which is already prepared, in packets or tins, or often frozen. People also go to fast-food restaurants a lot, where they buy take-away meals.

(b) This type of food is very **convenient** in the busy, modern world, but it often **contains** a lot of chemical additives, or a lot of fat or sugar.

(c) If you eat a lot of sugar, dentists say you might get **cavities** in your teeth.

(d) Similarly, if you eat a lot of salt, doctors will tell you that this is bad for your heart.

(e) Most health experts will say that the best food is fresh, natural food such as fruit and vegetables. They also say that we should cut down on the amount of fat we eat. **Nowadays** we eat too much oil and butter. Instead of frying food in fat, we should lightly boil it, steam it or eat it raw, as in salads.

(f) Food which hasn't been cooked often contains more vitamins. These vitamins are often destroyed in the **process** of cooking.

(g) Of course, it is as we get older that we start to notice the effects of bad eating habits. When we're young, we don't have to worry too much, but it's a good idea to develop good eating habits as early in life as possible.

3 Can you match these questions to the paragraph which answers them?

1 Why is uncooked food often better for us? ☐

2 What's wrong with convenience food? ☐

3 What type of food do people eat these days? ☐

4 Are good eating habits important for both young and older people? ☐

5 How can salt affect us? ☐

6 What's wrong with eating a lot of sugar? ☐

7 What do health experts advise us to eat? ☐

4 Match the words with what they mean.

cavities ⌐ not cooked
additives ⌐ little holes in your teeth
raw   as cold as ice
frozen   something found naturally in food that is good for us
vitamins   something added to food to give it more flavour or colour

5 Who do you think says these things?

I like fast-food because I'm always in a hurry.

If my children eat properly now they might not have health problems later.

If you eat too many sweets you will have to visit me often.

Too much salt can cause troubles for your heart.

a   b

c   d

6 Can you finish these sentences?

1 Too much salt is bad for us because _____

2 Sugar is bad for our teeth because _____

3 Butter and oil _____

4 Fresh salads _____

23

12 Tony's day

1 Can you fill in the gaps with the correct word?

present simple   present continuous

simple past

2 Read about Tony's day.

1 We use the _____ to talk about what we are doing now.

2 We use the_____ to talk about what we usually do or facts that do not change.

3 We often use the_____ _____ to talk about things that happened in the past, but are not happening now.

Tony's day starts at 7.15 am when his father wakes him up by shouting "Breakfast's ready" at the top of his voice.

Breakfast's ready!

He yawns, **stretches** and gets out of bed slowly. He goes downstairs to the kitchen. Tony always has toast with jam for breakfast.

By 8 am he's ready for school. He says goodbye to his parents and sets off. He meets his friends at the train station. He says hello to Sean, Jennifer and Caroline. They never **shake hands**. English people only really shake hands with people they meet for the first time. Young people rarely shake hands. The train comes in at 8.10.

After 10 minutes they reach the next town, Faversham. This is where the school is. They get off the train and walk to school. They always go the same way. In fact, it's a school rule that all pupils must walk the same way from the station to the school.

The streets are full of children wearing the same uniform. A black **blazer**, grey trousers for boys, blue skirts for girls, and white shirts with the school **tie** for everybody.

Tony usually arrives at school at 8.35. He walks fast. The bell goes at 8.45. The whole school (about 700 pupils and 30 teachers) meets in the **assembly** hall for morning prayers and **notices**.

Complete the table below with information from the text.

7.15   Tony's father wakes him up.

_____   He eats breakfast.

7.30   He has a shower and gets dressed.

8.00   _____

8.10   _____

_____   He arrives in Faversham.

8.35   _____

_____   The school bell rings.

_____   The school meeting begins.

4   Choose the best way to complete the following sentences.

1 Tony's father says "Breakfast's ready!"
   a quietly. ☐
   b loudly.   ☐
   c very loudly. ☐

2 Tony goes down to the kitchen
   a slowly. ☐
   b quickly. ☐
   c with lots of energy. ☐

3 Tony and his friends don't shake hands because
   a it's early in the morning. ☐
   b they're good friends already. ☐
   c they're too shy. ☐

4 The pupils
   a can go any way they like to school. ☐
   b must go the same way every day. ☐
   c must walk quickly. ☐

5 Girls and boys
   a wear the same uniform. ☐
   b must all wear a tie and blazer. ☐
   c can wear what they like. ☐

6 The school meeting every morning is for
   a 400 pupils and 30 teachers. ☐
   b the whole school. ☐
   c only the teachers. ☐

5 How does your school day begin? Do you have a similar daily routine to Tony or not? How is your morning different? Use the description of Tony's morning to write a description of your own. Begin like this.

My day starts at _____ , when I
_____
_____
_____

13   Tony's school

1 Without looking at Unit 12, write what you remember about Tony's day. Try to remember five things and compare your answers with a partner.

2 Now read about Tony's school.

After **assembly**, the pupils all go to their classes. The teacher arrives to call the **register**. He calls out everybody's surname and the children shout out "Here, sir!" when their names are called. Tony's surname is Young, so his name is the last on the register.

The first lesson begins at 9.15 am. There are seven lessons per day, each lasts 40 minutes. On Mondays, maths is the first lesson. Then comes PE (physical education). The class runs down to the changing rooms as quickly as possible. Almost everybody likes PE. For this lesson only, the boys and the girls are in separate classes.

Break is at 10.40 am. Tony has **tuck shop duty** on Mondays. He has to hurry to the tuck shop and sell biscuits and **crisps** to the other pupils. All fourth formers do tuck shop duties once or twice per term.

After break Tony's class has a double **biology** lesson. This is Tony's favourite subject. He's very interested in nature. Sometimes the whole class goes out to the countryside for a **wildlife** project.

Lunch is at 12.20 pm. The pupils go straight to the canteen and join the **queue** for lunch. Tony normally chooses a beefburger and chips. He's a **fussy** eater. He only really likes home cooking.

There are three more lessons in the afternoon: English, geography and history. Sometimes Tony finds it difficult to **concentrate** after lunch, so he usually sits at the back of the class, hoping the teachers won't notice him. The final bell rings at 3.30 pm. The pupils leap to their feet and start **packing up**. Before they leave, everybody must put their chairs up on the table, so that the cleaners can come straight in and clean.

Tony and his friends go to the station.

3 Find words in the text to match these pictures.

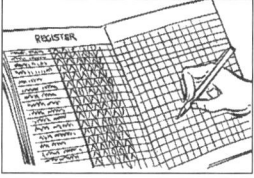

_____ _____

_____ _____

4 Choose the best way to complete these sentences.

1 Tony's name is last on the register because
   a Y is near the end of the alphabet. ☐
   b T is near the end of the alphabet. ☐
   c he's the youngest in the class. ☐

2 Boys and girls
   a are always in the same class. ☐
   b are usually separated. ☐
   c are in separate classes for PE only. ☐

3 Tony
   a sometimes has tuck shop duty. ☐
   b usually has tuck shop duty. ☐
   c always has tuck shop duty. ☐

4 Tony
   a likes most of the food in the canteen. ☐
   b prefers the food his mother and father cook. ☐
   c only eats beefburger and chips. ☐

5 Pupils put the chairs on the tables
   a to help the cleaners. ☐
   b because it looks tidy. ☐
   c for fun. ☐

5

There are many ways of expressing similarities. We can use the expressions **both** and **too**. For example:

We **both** have to wear uniform.

English school children wear uniform. We have to wear uniform, **too**.

We can explain differences using **but**. For example:

English school children have to wear uniform, **but** we don't.

Write six sentences comparing your school life to Tony's. Include things that are the same and things that are different. These headings might help:

Transport to school   Lunch and snacks
School subjects   School meetings
School uniform   Class times

27

14   The solar system

1 How many planets are there in our solar system? Close your books and see how many you can name.

2 Now read the text.

The solar system

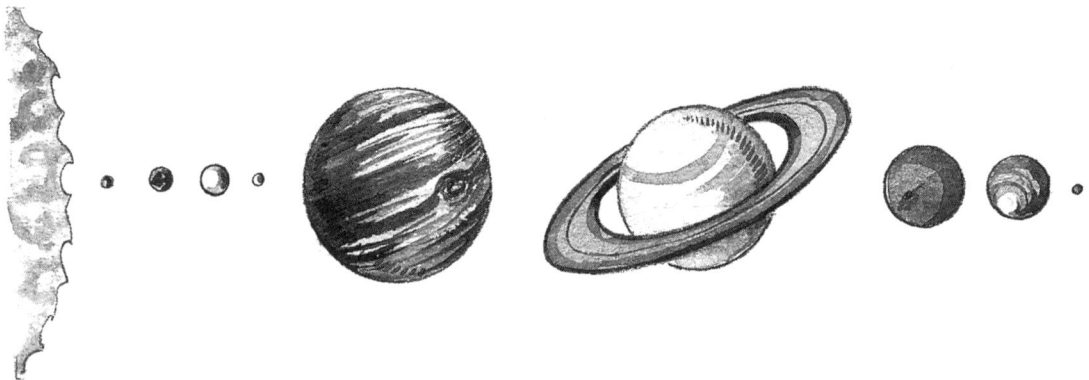

The moon and the stars are not the only objects shining in the sky. There are also **planets**. The sun has nine planets going around it. We live on one of these, the third planet from the sun – Earth.

The Earth moves around the sun once every year. It's about 150 million kilometres away from the sun. The planets that are nearer to the sun take less than a year to go round the sun once. Mercury is the closest to the sun, just 58 million kilometres away. Then comes Venus.

Planets that are further away from the sun take more than a year to **orbit** the sun. The most distant planet is Pluto. It takes over 247 years to go round the sun.

Planets do not send out their own heat or light like the sun. They shine in the sky only because the sun shines on them. They reflect the sun's light just like the moon does. The planets nearest to the sun are too hot to live on, while those furthest away are too cold. Living things would not be able to **survive** on these planets.

The biggest planet by far is Jupiter. It's larger than all the other planets put together. The most beautiful is Saturn, the sixth planet from the sun. Its beauty comes from the rings around it, which stretch for 65,000 kilometres.

3 Look at the table of facts. Some pieces of information are missing. Find them in the text and add them to the table.

_____	Neptune	Uranus	_____	_____	Mars	_____	108	_____
5,900	4,497	2,870	1,427	778	228		108	
_____	165	84	29	11.9	1.9	_____	0.6	0.2

4 Fill in the gaps with an adjective in the correct form.

1 Saturn is _____ from the sun than Jupiter. It's _____ in size than Uranus.
2 Uranus is _____ to the sun than Pluto, so Pluto takes _____ to orbit the sun than Uranus.
3 Jupiter is the _____ planet in the solar system.

Write three more sentences like these comparing two or more planets. Use the information in the text and in the table to help you.

5 Write out these sentences again putting the words in the right order and using the correct punctuation.

1 planets around sun are going there nine the
   There are nine planets going around the sun.
2 planet largest the is is while distant Pluto most sun Jupiter the the from

   _____

   _____

3 the the sun's moon light reflects

   _____

4 planets year take sun than round less Mercury two Venus and a to go the

   _____

   _____

29

Earthquakes - part one

1 See if you can answer the following questions.

1 What makes an earthquake happen?

2 What damage do earthquakes often cause?

3 Why do earthquakes occur in California?

4 How do we measure the size of an earthquake?

5 Can people always feel earthquakes?

6 Why did few people die in the 1994 Los Angeles earthquake?

2 Now read through the text and make sure your answers were right.

When there is an earthquake, the earth's surface **jumps** and **cracks**. This can make houses fall into very big holes, roads break up and the water in lakes disappear. Earthquakes happen when two **plates** in the earth's **crust jerk** against each other. The San Andreas fault in California is a point where two of these plates meet. There were recent earthquakes along the San Andreas fault in 1989 (in San Francisco) and 1994 (in Los Angeles).

The size and effect of every earthquake is measured on a scale from 1 to 10, called the **Richter scale**. A score of 8 or more on the Richter scale means damage to buildings and people is severe.

An earthquake measuring 3.4 or less is not usually felt, but is **recorded**. Some **instruments** can feel earthquakes thousands of miles away. Each year scientists record 800,000 earthquakes which are too small to be felt by people. At least 100 earthquakes a year damage buildings.

The 1994 earthquake in Los Angeles measured 6.6 on the Richter scale. It was strong enough to damage buildings, roads and bridges. Fortunately, not many people were killed by the earthquake. This is because it happened very early in the morning, while most people were still asleep in bed, rather than out on the streets of the city.

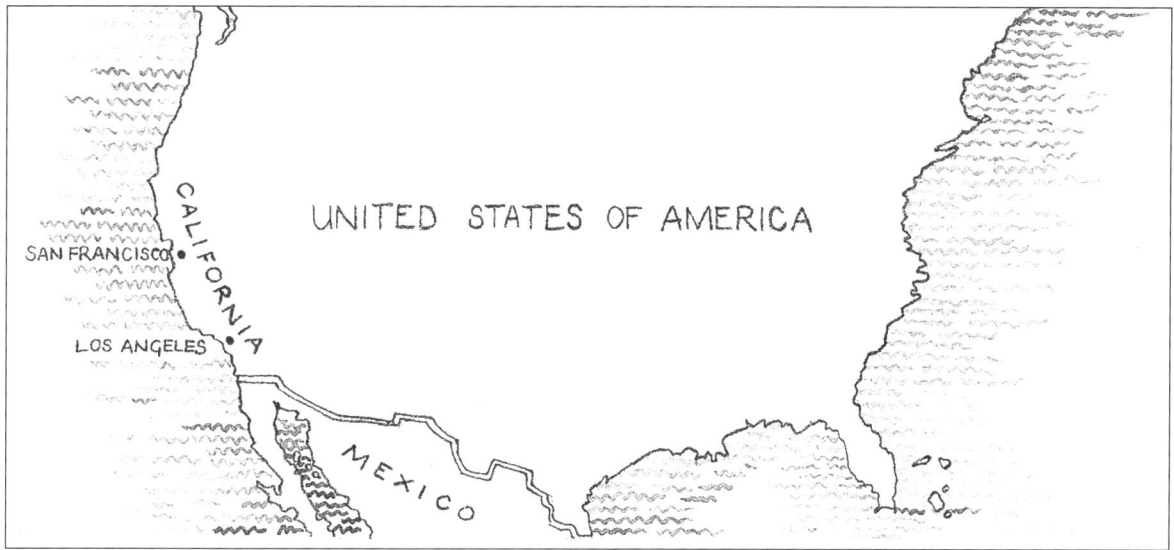

3 True (T) or false (F)?

1 The earth's surface doesn't move in
an earthquake. ☐

2 There was an earthquake in Los
Angeles in 1994. ☐

3 About 10 earthquakes a year cause
damage to buildings. ☐

4 Earthquakes are measured from
1 to 10 on the Richter scale. ☐

4 Imagine you were on holiday on a tropical
island. All of a sudden you felt an earthquake
of about 6.5 on the Richter scale. Write a
paragraph describing what happened. Use the
simple past tense. Include the answers to the
following questions.

1 Where were you when the earthquake happened?
2 What could you hear?
3 What could you see?
4 What did you do?
5 How did you feel?
6 How did you reach safety?
7 Were you alone?

31

1 After a serious earthquake what are the first things that need to be done to help survivors? Write a list of at least five things.

2 Now read the text and make a list of the things the charity Oxfam did with the money they raised to help the victims of the Indian earthquake.

In 1993 there was a terrible earthquake in Maharashtra, India. Oxfam, a charity that helps people worldwide, raised over £1 million from donations and was able to do a lot to help after the disaster.

One of the first things Oxfam did was to provide funds to buy food and blankets for the thousands of survivors.

Hundreds of **ordinary** people worked as volunteers and gave their time and energy to help clear rubble, **bury** the dead and comfort survivors. These people also received homes and food while they helped in the relief operation. One hotel was turned into a large, Oxfam-funded restaurant, where hungry helpers could go and get free meals.

Money was given from funds for school materials, health education, village meetings, organizing volunteers, **transport costs**, and for some necessary work to provide drinking water. Some of the money was spent on the job of **providing drainage and sanitation**.

Oxfam also gave funds and **assistance** to help people rebuild homes, hospitals and schools.

3

> Sometimes when you don't know a word, you can understand it by reading what goes before and after it.

Now choose the best meaning for the underlined words in the text.

1 donations
   a money given by people ☐
   b banks ☐
   c selling things ☐

2 funds
   a money raised ☐
   b help given ☐
   c work done ☐

3 survivors
   a children ☐
   b people who helped ☐
   c people who didn't die ☐

4 volunteers
   a workers who are very experienced ☐
   b workers who ask for a lot of money ☐
   c workers who don't ask to be paid ☐

5 rubble
   a streets and roads ☐
   b fallen stones and bricks ☐
   c rubbish ☐

6 relief operation
   a programme of education ☐
   b programme of help ☐
   c programme of entertainment ☐

7 drainage and sanitation
   a water systems ☐
   b food supplies ☐
   c help and money ☐

4 Which of these titles do you think is the best one for the text? Give them each a score of 1 to 4 (1 = best, 4 = worst). Explain why you have given them your score.

Help ☐
A bad time in Maharashtra ☐
How to handle an earthquake ☐
Oxfam's Maharashtra project ☐

Now write the best title (or one of your own) above the text.

5 Close your books. With your partner see how many of the words and expressions from the text you can remember. Now use the lists you wrote in exercise 1 to write a summary of how Oxfam helped in the earthquake.

17 Hobbies and spare time

1 Write down three of your hobbies. Compare them with your classmates. Have you chosen any of the same hobbies?

2 Now read about Toby's hobbies. Does he enjoy any of the same things as you and your classmates?

(a) I love playing volleyball. That's my sport. And I like to play **computer games** sometimes, but not too much. I also spend a lot of time **collecting** things. At the moment I collect coins and stamps from countries all over the world.

(b) My mother works in an international company, and they receive letters from all over the world. She **tears** the stamps off the envelopes and brings them home for me. I **steam** the stamps off the envelopes by holding them over hot water. You have to peel the stamp away from the paper slowly and carefully.

(c) I keep them in a stamp **album** which my Uncle Bob gave me for my birthday. I have a page for nearly every country in the world. My favourite ones are the Egyptian ones with the pictures of the Pyramids and the Sphinx, and the American ones with pictures of famous people like Elvis Presley.

(d) Coins are more difficult to find – I think that must be because people like to hold on to their money. On Saturdays I go with my Dad to a shop in my town. It's an **antique** shop. It sells mainly old furniture and **ornaments**. The man who owns the shop brings me a box of old coins and I choose the ones I like the best. There are some really old ones. I've got some old English coins with Queen Victoria on them.

(e) One of my friends collects some unusual things, like **bottle tops** and coloured **shoelaces** and things like that. She sticks them on to pieces of **cardboard** and makes collages. Some of them look really good.

3 Toby is in class 4G of St. Martin's School. Class 4K is doing a project on hobbies. Lauren interviewed Toby as part of the project. Can you match her questions below to Toby's answers above?

1 Where do you keep your stamps?
   I keep them in a stamp album.

2 How do you find all those interesting stamps?
   _____

3 What about coins? Are they easy to find?
   _____

4 What do you do in your spare time?
   _____

5 Do any of your friends have interesting collections? _____
   _____

4 When you interview someone you have to ask questions very clearly. Here are some of Toby's answers. Can you make the questions? The question word is there for you.

1 How _do you get the stamps off the envelopes_ ?
   I steam them off over hot water.
2 Which _____ ?
   The Egyptian ones.
3 Where _____ ?
   From an antique shop in town.
4 What _____ ?
   She makes collages.

5 Prepare some questions about hobbies and spare time to ask other pupils in your class. When you've finished, you can write a paragraph about one person's hobbies. Write questions to get information about what people like doing, what they need to do it, and also what they don't like doing.

1 How do you make a **kite**? If you think you know, tell your classmates.

2 Now read the text to see if you were right.

People enjoy themselves in many different ways when they go to the seaside. Apart from swimming, you often see people **paddling** at the edge of the water, canoeing, rowing, playing volleyball, or simply sunbathing. But if there's a strong sea **breeze**, it may be a little too fresh for sunbathing. That's when it's a good time to fly a kite.

Of course, you can buy beautiful kites in sports shops or toy shops, but do you know just how easy it is to make a kite? The answer is – very easy. Just follow the instructions below:

1 Glue two pieces of wood together and **twist** some **wire** round the **joint**. Cut **grooves** into the end of each piece of wood and tie string round the **frame**.

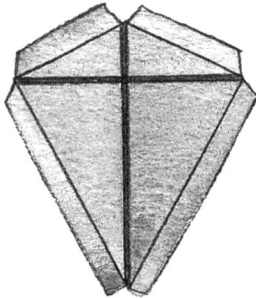

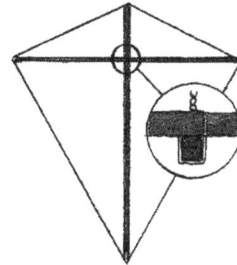

2 Cut a **diamond** shape from strong paper, 4 cm larger than the frame. Cut off the corners and then glue the paper down over the string.

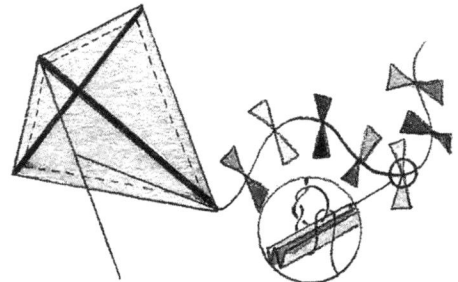

3 Make a tail from 4 m of string and coloured paper. Attach a piece of string 1.3 m long to the top and bottom of the kite. Attach the flying line to this. How much string do you think you need for the flying line?

3 There are a lot of beach activities mentioned in the first paragraph. Divide them into the two categories below:

Water activities	Land activities

4 1 Match the words in the box to the pictures.

wire   joint   groove   string   to glue

1

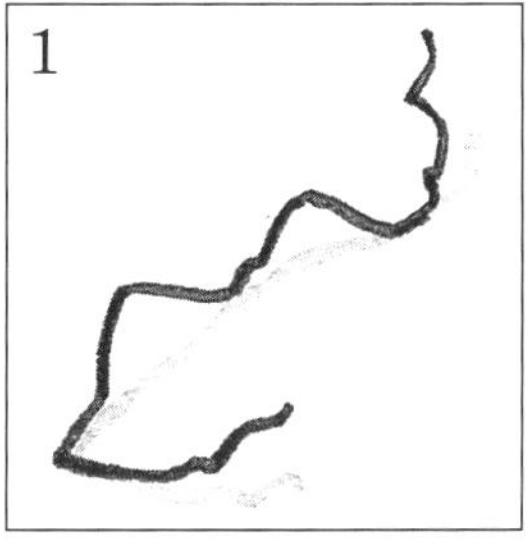

2

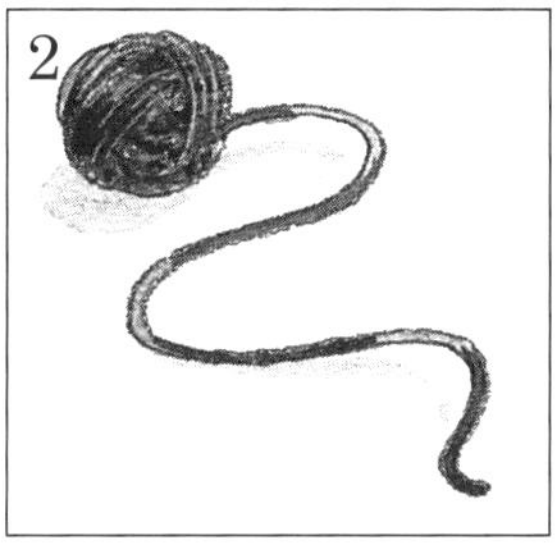

_____   _____

3

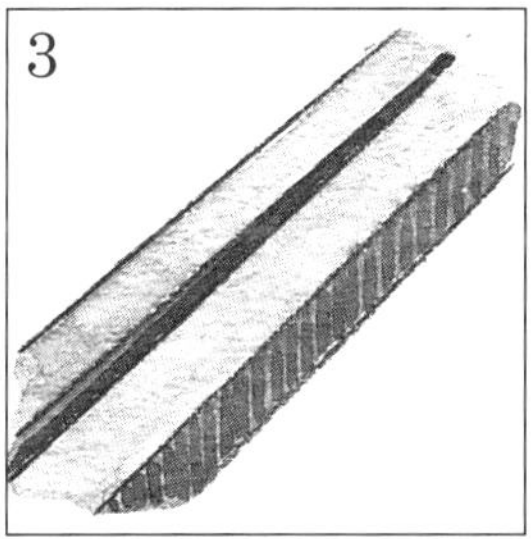

_____

4

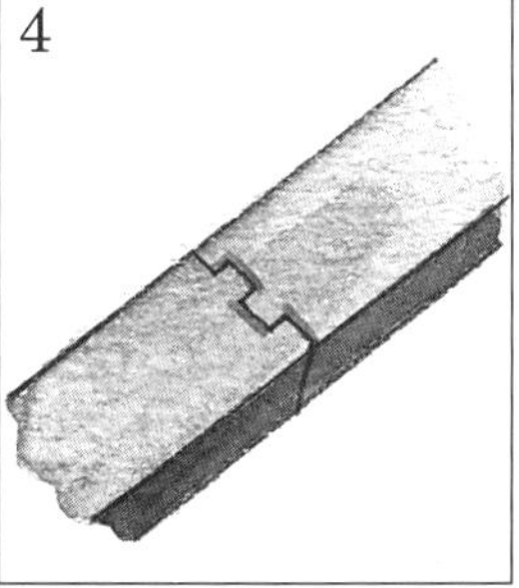

5

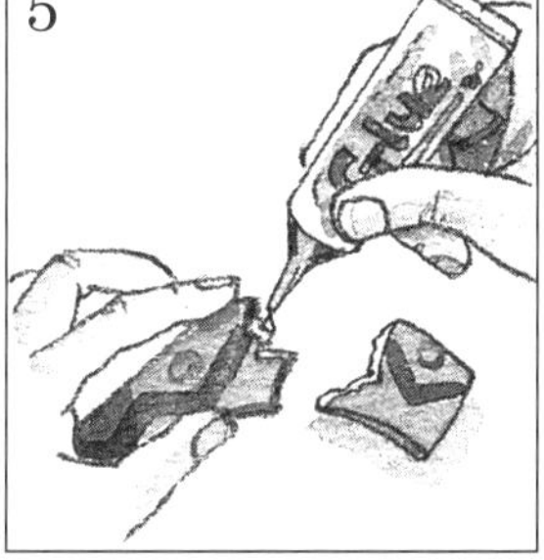

_____   _____

2 What other things will you need to make the kite? Can you make a list of everything (e.g. scissors)?

5

Look at the kite. Can you write the instructions for the decorations? Remember to use the infinitive form, like in the text in exercise 2.

In the top right section, draw a circle
with a triangle inside
_____
_____
_____
_____
_____
_____
_____
_____
_____
_____
_____
_____

1 Write down as many **grammatical structures** as you can in 30 seconds. How many did you find? Compare them with the class.

2

What is grammar? Some people hate it. Some people love it. Whatever you think about it, it is an important part of language.

Grammar is the way we put words together to say something that **makes sense**. If you want people to understand what you mean, you have to use the right kinds of words. *The drive of the car fell asleep in his sitting.* Two words are wrong here. What are they?

Grammar is also about putting words in the right order. ***He the cake ate*** is not correct because the words are in the wrong order. How should we say it?

We have grammatical names for different groups of words. **Nouns** name things or people: for example, biscuit, car, woman, teacher. Can you think of some more nouns? **Verbs** tell you what someone is doing or what is happening: for example, walk, run, cry, speak. Can you think of some more verbs? **Adjectives** describe things: for example, pretty, big, long, nice. Can you think of some more adjectives?

We call these different groups **parts of speech**. We put parts of speech together to make sentences. Nearly all sentences have a verb and most have nouns.

3 Find the questions in the text and answer them with your partner.

For example:

Question: What is grammar?

Answer: Grammar is the way we put words together to say something that makes sense.

4 These sentences have words in the wrong order. Can you correct them?

1 Most kinds of fish lay numbers huge of eggs.

   Most kinds of fish lay huge
   numbers of eggs.

2 Finland has winters long cold and summers warm.

   _____
   _____

3 On the coast of Ireland in the fishing industry many people work.

   _____
   _____
   _____

4 Pandas giant are some of the rarest animals in the world.

   _____
   _____

5 Louis Pasteur discovered that cause disease bacteria.

   _____
   _____

6 In the Middle East farmers cotton, tobacco and fruits such as dates, grapes, oranges and olives grow.

   _____
   _____

5 Put the words in the box below into the right columns.

produce word earth year good slow electricity build glass attack explode move rich put sand pure

Nouns	Adjectives	Verbs

6 Find all the grammar and punctuation terms in this wordsearch.

```
P A R A G R A P H C A T S
N O U N T R E E C O M M A
D O G V E R B A R O U N D
S E N T E N C E G A T E S
B O O K S F U L L S T O P
C A P I T A L L E T T E R
Q U E S T I O N M A R K I
T O P S P E E C H M A R K
```

1 Read the text below, and decide which of these titles would be the best one for it. Then write it beside the unit number above.

a Making a camera ☐
b The history of cameras ☐
c Understanding cameras ☐

(a) Most families have a camera. A family picnic, a party or a holiday wouldn't be the same without photos of people gathered in front of the camera all saying 'cheese'. But have you ever wondered how a camera works?

(b) When you take a picture with a camera, the **lens** takes in light from the person or scene you are photographing. The light makes a small, upside-down image on the film inside. Film is **sensitive** to light, so it must be kept in darkness until it is **processed** and the finished photographs are developed. The **shutter** is **set** so the camera lets in the same amount of light whether it is dull or sunny.

(c) The first real camera was made by a Frenchman called Joseph Niepce in 1826. His camera produced a picture on a metal plate. In 1947, Edwin Land from America invented a camera that produced instant photos.

(d) Making a camera is a **complicated** process. However, it is easy for you to make a **pin-hole viewer**, which works on exactly the same **principle** as a camera. Just follow these simple instructions:

1 Take a cardboard **tube**.

2 Cover one end with **foil**.

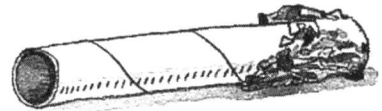

3 Cover the other end with **tracing paper**.

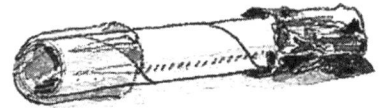

4 **Shade** this end with extra card.

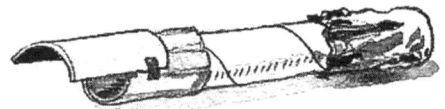

5 Make a large pin-hole in the middle of the foil.

6 Point the viewer at a bright window (but never point it directly at the sun).

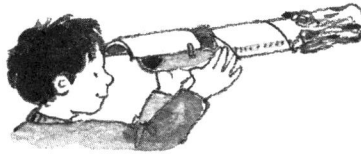

2 True (T) or false (F)?

1 People say 'cheese' in front of cameras because they're hungry. `F`

2 Light enters the camera through the lens. ☐

3 Light can damage film. ☐

4 More light enters the camera during sunny weather. ☐

5 Edwin Land invented the camera. ☐

6 A pin-hole viewer gives us a good idea of how a camera works. ☐

7 Light enters the viewer through the tracing paper. ☐

3 Now find these words in the text and decide if you think a, b or c is the best meaning.

1 gathered (paragraph a line 4)
   a together, in a group ☐
   b smiling ☐
   c standing ☐

2 image (paragraph b line 5)
   a shadow ☐
   b picture ☐
   c hole ☐

3 dull (paragraph b line 12)
   a opposite of 'bright' ☐
   b rainy ☐
   c evening ☐

4 instant (paragraph c line 7)
   a on paper ☐
   b colour ☐
   c ready immediately ☐

4 Use the instructions in exercise 1 to make a pin-hole viewer. Then write about what you did, and what you saw. Use the following words to help you.

First . . . .   but . . . .   Then . . . .
Next . . . .   After that . . . .
and . . . .   Finally . . . .

You could start like this:

First we took an old cardboard tube and we covered one end of it with kitchen foil. Then ...

Oxford University Press
Great Clarendon Street, Oxford OX2 6DP

Oxford New York
Auckland Bangkok Buenos Aires Cape Town Chennai
Dar es Salaam Delhi Hong Kong Istanbul Karachi Kolkata
Kuala Lumpur Madrid Melbourne Mexico City Mumbai Nairobi
São Paulo Shanghai Singapore Taipei Tokyo Toronto

with an associated company in Berlin

Oxford and *Oxford English* are trade marks of
Oxford University Press

ISBN 0 19 312004 6

© Oxford University Press 1995

First published 1995
Fourth impression 2002

Illustrations by Oxford Illustrators and Shelagh McNicholas

Cover by Sue Vaudin

Designed and typeset by Pentacor

Printed in China